DUDLEY SCHOOLS
LIBRARY SERVICE

KU-455-336

Schools Library and Information Services

S00000796180

Life Around the World
Homes in Many Cultures

Heather Adamson

raintree
a Capstone company — publishers for children

Raintree is an imprint of Capstone Global Library Limited, a company incorporated in England and Wales having its registered office at 264 Banbury Road, Oxford, OX2 7DY – Registered company number: 6695582

www.raintree.co.uk
myorders@raintree.co.uk

Text © Capstone Global Library Limited 2017
The moral rights of the proprietor have been asserted.

All rights reserved. No part of this publication may be reproduced in any form or by any means (including photocopying or storing it in any medium by electronic means and whether or not transiently or incidentally to some other use of this publication) without the written permission of the copyright owner, except in accordance with the provisions of the Copyright, Designs and Patents Act 1988 or under the terms of a licence issued by the Copyright Licensing Agency, Saffron House, 6–10 Kirby Street, London EC1N 8TS (www.cla.co.uk). Applications for the copyright owner's written permission should be addressed to the publisher.

Edited by Sarah L Schuette
Designed by Alison Thiele
Picture research by Kara Birr
Originated by Capstone Global Library Ltd
Printed and bound in China

ISBN 978 1 4747 3535 3
20 19 18 17 16
10 9 8 7 6 5 4 3 2 1

British Library Cataloguing in Publication Data
A full catalogue record for this book is available from the British Library.

Acknowledgements
Shutterstock: Blaz Kure, Cover, czardases, 17, f9photos, 15, Greg and Jan Ritchie, 19, Israel Hervas Bengochea, 13, Lakis Fourouklas, 1, Marc Dietrich, 21, Michael G Smith, 5, photoBeard, 11, Pichugin Dmitry, 9, Simon Krzic, 7

Every effort has been made to contact copyright holders of material reproduced in this book. Any omissions will be rectified in subsequent printings if notice is given to the publisher.

All the Internet addresses (URLs) given in this book were valid at the time of going to press. However, due to the dynamic nature of the Internet, some addresses may have changed, or sites may have changed or ceased to exist since publication. While the author and publisher regret any inconvenience this may cause readers, no responsibility for any such changes can be accepted by either the author or the publisher.

DUDLEY SCHOOLS LIBRARY SERVICE	
S00000796180	
£11.99	J643
15-Mar-2017	PETERS

Contents

Places to live

Big or small. Short or tall.
Homes are safe places
to rest and play.

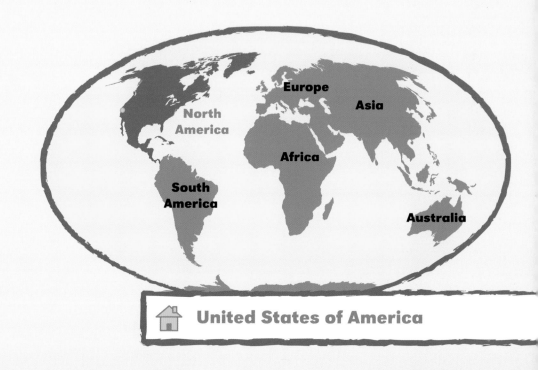

North America

Europe

Asia

Africa

South America

Australia

🏠 United States of America

Kinds of homes

Cabins have thick walls
to keep out the cold.

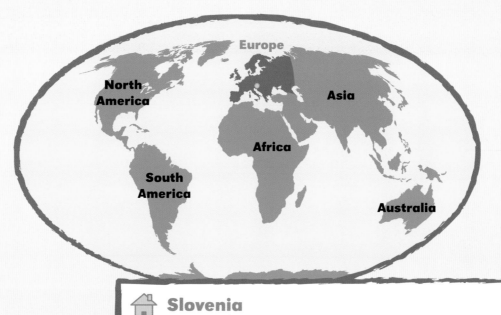

🏠 Slovenia

Huts have grass roofs
to keep off the rain.

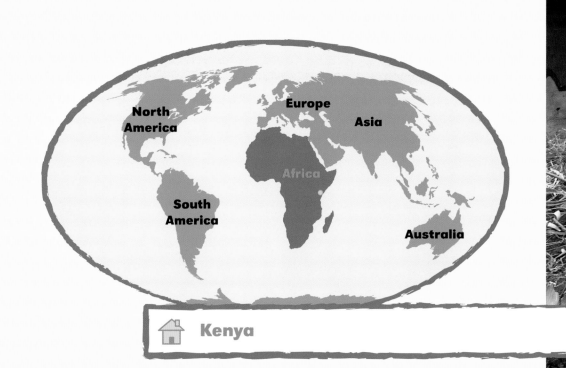

🏠 Kenya

Adobe homes
are made of clay.
Clay stays cool
in the hot desert sun.

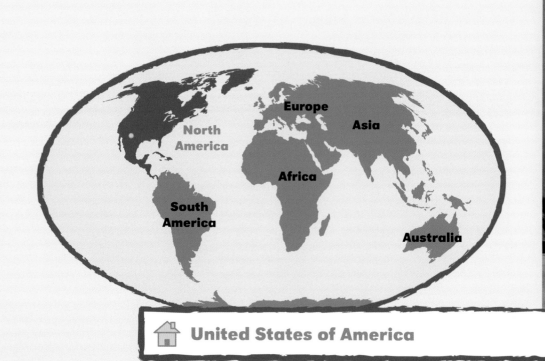

🏠 United States of America

Stilt houses are
built above rivers
to keep water out.

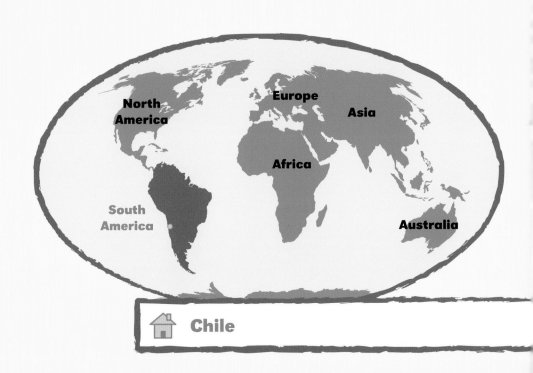

North America

Europe

Asia

Africa

South America

Australia

🏠 Chile

Houseboats are
floating homes that sail
up and down rivers.

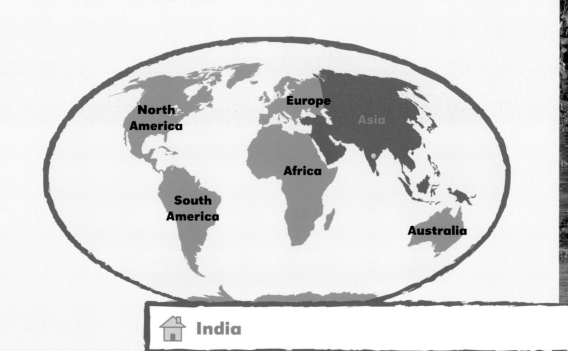

 India

City and country

Big cities have blocks of flats where lots of families live.

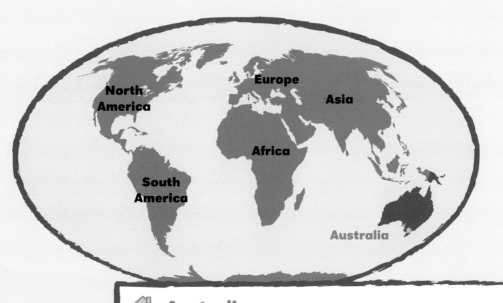

 Australia

Country farms have
lots of land where
one family's home sits.

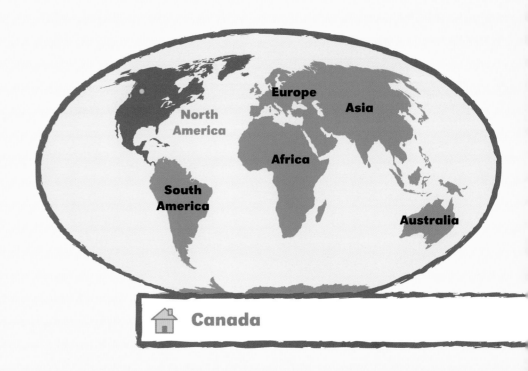

Canada

Your home

The world has
all kinds of homes.
What's your home like?

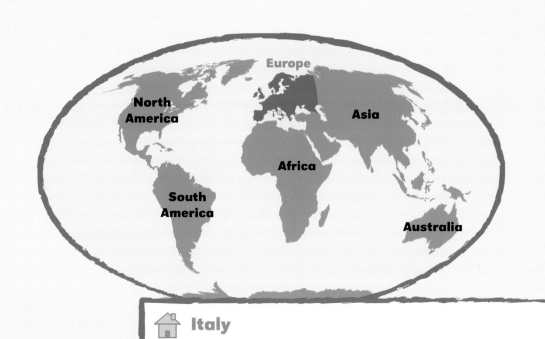

Europe

North America

Asia

Africa

South America

Australia

🏠 Italy

Glossary

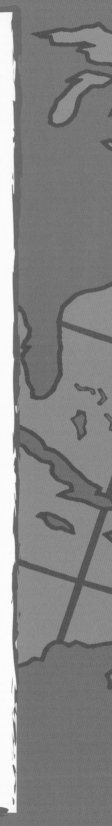

adobe   brick material made from clay mixed with straw and dried in the sun

cabin   small, simple house made of wood

clay   kind of earth that can be shaped when wet and baked to make bricks or pottery

farm   area of land used for growing crops or raising animals

hut   small house often made from sticks, grass or mud

stilt   one of the posts that holds a building above the ground or water

Find out more

Home Around the World, Kate Petty (Frances Lincoln Children's Books, 2007)

Homes Around the World (Children Like Us), Moira Butterfield (Wayland, 2016)

If You Lived Here: Houses of the World, Giles Laroche (Houghton Mifflin, 2011)

Websites

http://www.kidcyber.com.au/houses-around-the-world/

Fun facts about homes around the world.

http://www.bbc.co.uk/education/clips/z3xsb9q

A video about different climates and the houses people build there.

Index

24